CW00571961

HORSE RACE BETTING

HOW TO MAKE IT PAY

BY ROBIN "BIRDIE" CROW

www.myhorseracingsystems.co.uk

Eclipse Racing Publications

ISBN: 978-1-52396-902-9

Contents

Welcome

Section One

Here's your fish

Section Two

Here's how to fish

Welcome

Horse racing is called "The Sport of Kings" but since those first matches between aristocrat's horses racing across Newmarket Heath it has also become the sport of "the common man". Although out of respect for political correctness I suppose we should say "the common man or woman".

We the lesser mortals may not aspire to own a Derby winner or Gold Cup steeple chaser but we still liked to be involved in the sport by going to the races or watching it on television. We also show our support by pouring millions of pounds every day into the ever-welcoming pockets of the bookmakers and betting exchanges.

Why do we do this? It is because we are looking to make a profit on our bets and take more away from the bookies and exchanges than we put in. Sadly 95% of us fail to do this on any kind of regular basis.

The truth is that it is the bookies that continually come out ahead of the punter. This is not really surprising when you consider the facts. The days of the corner street bookmaker are almost over and a few big High Street players now control the industry. These companies are highly efficient businesses that employ thousands of specialists whose ultimate task is to help their companies show a profit. There are accountants, lawyers, odds compilers, marketers, public relations, media experts and many others employed to ensure that the bookies win and the punter loses.

How can the average punter compete? The truth is the "average" punter can't because he is approaching his betting in the wrong way. If you are wondering what my definition of the average punter is, it is simply all of those in the 95% bracket who regularly come second in the bookie/punter race.

In this book I want to demonstrate how it is possible by building up your knowledge and changing both your approach and mindset to your horse race betting you can become one of the 5% who make profits from their activities.

What I do not want you to do is risk any of your own money putting my suggestions to the test. For that reason the first few pages of this book I will outlines a method by which you can establish a betting pot of £1000 or more. The two best points about this method are that it is totally risk free and you will be delighted to know that the money will be coming from the pockets of your friendly online bookmakers.

What you do with the money once you have it is entirely up to you but I hope that you will apply the lessons on profitable betting that I outline in Section Two.

The only thing that I ask is that you remember there is no such animal as "a sure thing". Please bet responsibly and never wager more than you can afford to lose.

Whatever you decide to do with the money, spend it or invest it in your Betting Business I wish you good luck.

Robin "Birdie" Crow

Section 1

"Here's your fish"

How to Turn £50 into £1000+ Risk Free

This book does not contain some secret system that will guarantee that every horse you back is a winner or that every day you back horses you will show a profit. If you believe such a thing exists then you are living in cloud cuckoo land. However, what this book does contain is a method by which you can build up a sizeable betting bank of £1000 or more with no risk to your own finances. By now I hope you realise by simply reading this section you can be a winner, for the price of this book you will be shown how to get £1000 or more straight from the online bookies pockets. What is even better is that you can do it without any real risk to your own cash.

Section One is the smallest part of the book because building your sizeable betting pot is the easy part. Once you have accumulated enough money you can start the serious business of making your horse race betting pay. Getting the

£1000 + will not happen overnight and may take a month or two but you can spend this time studying Section Two after which you will possibly change your whole perspective on how to profitably bet on horse races. All of this is covered in Section Two and requires some work and effort on your part. If you are not prepared to put this effort in then do not worry just follow the information in section one and take the £1000+ and run. I shall be sorry if you do that because you will be passing up the opportunity of making a regular income straight out of the bookmaker's pockets but that is entirely up to you.

"If you give a man a fish you feed him for a day, teach him to fish and you have fed him for life"

An old proverb

In other words It is more worthwhile to teach someone to do something than to do it for them and that is what I hope to do for you. I have no "winning system" to give or sell you but I think I can show you how to seriously improve your chances of joining the 5 percent of successful punters.

In this book Section One is the fish, Section Two is were I teach you to fish.

To begin I am going to show you how you build up a betting bank from around £50 up to £500 or £1,000 with no financial risk to yourself. The only real factor that affects the amount of "free" money you can make depends on whether you already have any accounts with some online bookmakers.

The process is very straightforward and easy to understand and providing you follow the simple rules you should be able to build up your betting pot in a relatively short time. The competition for your business amongst online bookmakers is fierce and as a result they are nearly all prepared to offer bonuses in the form of free bets to encourage you to register and bet with them. Bookies do not give you the free bets because they have had a sudden attack of generosity but because they know that the average punter will not only lose his free bet but go on to lose much more of his or her own money. This will not happen to you because if you follow the betting method outlined in this book you will be regularly taking money from the bookmaker instead of consistently giving him yours. Of course the real bonus is that to do this you will be using the bookmakers money, a real win-win situation

The online bookmakers bonus offers.

Online bookmaking is a profitable business and is highly competitive. To attract new business (in other words punters cash) they nearly all make very good bonus offers. To keep to the fishing analogy they see it as *"a sprat to catch a mackerel".* Yet I am going to show you how to catch a net full of *sprats that you can use to* build up a betting bank of £1000 or more. The actual amount that you can make using my method has just a couple of limitations. If you already have several accounts with online bookmakers you will not be able to claim all the new customer bonuses so this may reduce the overall total that you can make. Currently there is around £2000 in total available from the current online bookmaker's bonus offers.

It is worth remembering that bookmakers are not fools and as more and more people take advantage of these bonus offers and then take the money and run they will change the rules. There are already signs that this is happening so I would not wait too long before you start to take advantage of the offers.

What do I need before I can start?

As we are dealing with online bookmakers you will need a computer, tablet or phone with Internet access. I use my laptop for most of my online betting although when I am away from home I use my i-Pad for most activities. You will also need to set up a Betfair account at www.betfair.co.uk. I suspect that most readers will be familiar with how Betfair works but if not there is some good "how to" information on the Betfair site.

Where do you find these bonus offers?

You can of course simply use your web browser to find online bookmakers and go from site to site to see what they offer but a better option is to go to

www.top100bookmakers.com/signup.php

where you find not only a list of online bookmakers but details of their current offers and a direct link to their sites.

There are other sites you may also visit to find online bookmakers bonuses.

www.olbg.com/free.php

www.fre-bet-advice.com

www.freebetsources.com

As you will see the offers vary from a £10 bonus right up to sites offering up to £200 in free bets. A good plan is to start with the lowest offers and work your way up to the higher. By doing this you do not need to put very much of your own money to get started although you will be able to withdraw your own investment after a very short time.

Online Bookmakers Bonus Offers

Most bonus offers consist of offering a free bet up to a specific amount usually dependent upon how much you deposit to open your account. A typical offer might be a free bet of 50% of your deposit after your first bet up to a set limit. So if you deposit £100 after first bet you would have a free bet of £50.

Now the task we have is to convert the free bets into real cash without risking our own money. To do this we are going to use the largest and most successful betting exchange site, www.betfair.co.uk.

The introduction of Betting Exchanges back in the late nineties heralded a new dawn in betting. For the first time punters were given the opportunity not only to back on an events outcome, a horse coming first, a football team winning a match or a snooker player getting the trophy but could also lay a bet on this not happening. An important point to remember is that Betfair is not a bookmaker but simply middleman who brings those who wish to back an outcome together with those who wish to lay the opposing outcome. For this Betfair takes a commission, initially 5% so they cannot lose and if you follow the following method neither can you.

When you open your Betfair account, if you do not already have one, you will need to deposit some money into that account before you can begin trading. It does not have to be a great deal and as little £30 will be enough to start and you should recover this in a matter of days. You will also need at last £10 or £20 to open your first online bookmakers accounts.

It may surprise you but for this cash raising method we are not going to be betting on horse racing. For this particular plan we need to bet on two teams or individuals playing each other. Football, snooker and tennis can be ideal for this. In snooker and tennis a player can only lose and in soccer if you have backed a side to win and they lose or draw then that is a losing bet.

As you are reading a book about horseracing you may not know anything about the other sports but this does not matter. In fact many of my bets when using this method were on foreign football matches between teams that I had never heard of and in countries I knew nothing about. The only requirement is that your bookmaker and Betfair have a market for that event.

If you use this method you cannot lose, but that does come with one caveat. You must study the terms and conditions of the offers you take up and understand any restrictions they impose. Before we move on to the plan it is important that you understand that these "free" bets do not come without strings attached. Normally you will have to make a "qualifying bet" with your own money before you can claim your "free" bet. Also you cannot draw the bookies bonus until you have had a bet with it.

There are three types of offer you may encounter and it is important that you understand the differences between the three.

Deposit Bonus. With this offer you will be required to deposit a sum of money with the bookmaker and in return he will increase your deposit with a percentage bonus, often 50%. If you deposit £20 he will add a bonus of £10. With these offers to make the most you should go for the maximum possible. For example if the offer is

50% up to a maximum of £50 you should deposit £100. After all why just make £10 when for the same effort you can make £50?

There will be conditions to the offer, you may have to make a certain number of bets before you can withdraw your winnings. There may also be a restriction on the prices, for instances all your bets may have to be placed at odds of 1.5 (2/1 on) or greater. All of these restrictions will be laid out in the bookmaker's terms and conditions.

Standard or Matched Free Bet. In this case you deposit some money with the online bookmaker and you use it to place your first bet. The bookmaker then gives you a free bet to the same amount. So if your first bet is £50 whether it wins or loses you will get a free bet of £50. Again it is important to read the terms and conditions before opening an account.

Risk Free Bet. These days there are very few, if any, of these offers around but the basic idea is that the bookmaker offers to refund your stake if your first bet loses.

How can we profit from these offers?

Deposit Bonus Offers. With this type of offer all you have to do is back an event with the bookmaker and then at similar or near similar odds lay the opposing outcome on Betfair. The secret, if there is one, is to find an event where the bookmaker is offering the same or near same odds as Betfair are giving as their lay price for the same event. You definitely do not want anything where the odds difference is greater that 0.10.

For this method you should look at events that provide a simple win/lose result such as tennis, snooker or football. (In football a draw is considered a losing result if you have backed a team to win) The one sport not to use is horse racing because the prices can fluctuate so quickly that between backing and laying the price may well go outside our acceptable limits.

An example would be if you deposit £50 and the bookmaker adds £25 to your account. You back a result for the full £75 and lay the same outcome on Betfair for £75.

If the bet loses you have won £75 from Betfair (less 5% commission) and lost £50 at the bookmakers. If the bet wins you have the profit from that bet in your bookmakers account but have lost £75 on Betfair. You will have to meet any wagering requirements before you can withdraw your winnings. With these follow up bets you must make sure that the winnings cover any liability you may have with Betfair which they will do if both prices are or are nearly the same.

This way you will come out with a profit whatever happens. If the initial bet loses it will save you any further effort with that particular account. Although the most important point is to ensure near matching odds it is also worth favouring bets that you think may possibly lose rather than backing near certainties. It can save unnecessary work but never do this if the odds are more than 0.10 apart.

Standard or Matched Free Bets. In the case of a Standard or Matched Free Bet you are required to place one or more bets to qualify for a free bet. With this first bet all you are looking for is to break even so again you simply look for an opportunity where the back and lay options are closely priced. Once this event is over you will have the free bet. You then repeat the process backing the full amount with the bookmaker and placing a lay bet on Betfair. If the bet wins you then withdraw the money and if it has lost the money will already be in your Betfair account.

Because it is so important I am going to emphasize again that you should look carefully at the "terms and conditions" of the bonus offer. Read the details carefully   and ensure that you fully understand what you have to do to get your free bet and how and when you can withdraw the money. There is one company for instance that has what appears a very generous offer but they requires you to make five bets of your own before you can access the "free" money. Sites with conditions like that should be avoided

The amount of the bonus varies but most of those that do not have restrictive conditions seem to offer free bets of between £20 and £50. You should note that this figure will be a maximum and is dependent upon you depositing a similar amount with them. So if the bookie is advertising a maximum of a £20 bonus and you only deposit £10 then your "free" bet will only be £10 and if you do not go for the maximum bonus you are passing money by.

The next step is to find a game or match in which the odds for a team or player are over evens and below 2.5 decimal odds to win. . Next check the Betfair price for the reverse result to see if it is close to the bookies win odds.

Here is an example:

Tonight as I write this Dynamo Kiev are going to play Florentina in European Cup Match. The odds with most of the bookmakers are 2.4 on Dynamo to win and Betfair are 2.5 on them losing. So we could have a bet.

Assuming the bookie is offering a £20 "free" bet after your qualifying bet place £20 to win of Dynamo with them. Now go to Betfair and place £20 on the Exchange for Dynamo to lose.

The outcome will be if Dynamo wins you will win £28 and you will be now qualified for your free bet but will have lost £30 on Betfair which means your free £20 bet has cost you £2.

If Dynamo loses then you will have lost £20 to the bookie but still have your free bet and you will have made £19.50 in your Betfair account (£20-5%) in which case your free bet has only cost 50p.

Even in the worse situation i.e. Dynamo win then you will have lost £30 from your Betfair account. But there are no worries; as you will soon get it back (with interest) As Dynamo won you now have £48 in your bookmaker's account plus a "free" £20 bet with the bookie.

The next step is to find another suitable match or game and repeat the process. Back the side priced between 2/1 and 4/1 with the bookie using your "free" bet. But now we have to do a little mathematical calculation. First you need to understand why this is.

Stake £20 on Betfair and with the bookie

Odds Backed at 2.4 to win laid at 2.5 to lose

Result	Betfair Account	Bookies Account
1st Bet wins	-£30	£28 + £20 Stake
1st Bet loses	£19.50	-£20 (+free bet)

At this point you will have to deposit some funds into your Betfair account. The actual amount will depend upon the price of the next bet. I recommend looking for a bet between 2/1 (3.0) and 4/1 (5.0). This should give you the best return. You could just back and lay even amounts i.e. back £20 (the free bet) and lay £20 but it is just possible if you do this you could lose some money. Now we move on to use the Bookies "free" bet.

Stake £20 on Betfair and with the Bookie

Odds backed 3/1 (4.00) to win 4.1 to lose

Result	Betfair Account	Bookies Account	Profit/Loss
1st Bet wins 2nd Bet wins	-£90	£88	-£2
1st Bet wins 2nd Bet loses	-£10.50	£28	£17.50
1st Bet loses 2nd Bet wins	-£42.50	£88	£45.50
1st Bet loses 2nd Bet loses	£39	-£20	£19

Note :A win is when it is a successful bet with the bookie and a loss is when it is successful lay bet on Betfair.

In the first example where both bets are wins with the bookies but losing lays on Betfair you will make a small lose. There are two options, you either accept this risk or an alternative to cut out any risk is to calculate a lower amount to lay on Betfair to ensure that you cannot make a loss. Of course by doing this you are lowering your potential profit but you only need to consider this in the case of your first bet being a winner. (Your bet wins with the bookie but loses on Betfair).

To ensure a profit in this case where the first bet won with the bookie you need to work out the correct stake to lay so that you will make a profit. In this case if you back at £20 but only lay £18 the result would be:

Result	Betfair Account	Bookies Account
2nd Bet wins	-£85.80	£88
2nd Bet loses	-£12.90	£28

Risk Free Bet

In this type of promotion the bookmaker offers to replace your stake should your first bet lose. Although this type of bonus does sometime appear they seem to becoming less common and I have not seen such an offer for quite a while. If the do reappear the basic idea is that if you bet say £25 and your bet loses the bookie will credit the amount of your first bet back to your account and you can withdraw it if you wish. Basically this really is a free bet which is perhaps why the bookies no longer offer it.

You can continue to use method to build up your betting bank until you run out of bookies. Another good point which I have noticed is that even after you have used your free bet and moved on to other bookmakers you will continue to get further bonus offers from some firms and you can use these to your advantage.

Here are the points to remember

- ALWAYS READ THE BOOKMAKERS TERMS AND

CONDITIONS REGARDING "FREE" BETS BEFORE

DEPOSITING MONEY.

- Bet only on two outcome events (win or lose) such as soccer, tennis and snooker. (Never horse racing!!)
- For backing and laying find the odds that are closest together and compare the odds.
- Keep records of all your bets. Also when registering with a new online bookmaker keep a note of your username and password. It will make it easier for you later.
- Set up a separate email address specifically for your betting activities. Once you start registering with bookmakers you are going to be inundated with offers and spam which would only swamped your normal email account.

Using the bookmaker's bonuses is the easiest risk free way to build up a decent betting bank that will help you achieve your aim of making your betting pay. It may seem a little confusing at first but study the idea and have a couple of dry runs to see how you would have fared and then go for it as there is nothing to lose.

You now have a simple method you can use to build up a bank of £1000+, which can either be used as your betting bank or you can simply take the money and run. If you take the second option there is no need for you to read any more as you have already got a very good return for the price you paid for the book or an even a better return if you borrowed it from friend.

However, there are a couple of points to understand about this method, firstly, it will only work if you are based in the United Kingdom. Secondly, bookmakers as a group are not known for a willingness to give money away and as more people come to realize the potential of the bonus offer they may make the terms and conditions more restrictive so do not delay if you want to use the method.

It should take between one and two months for you to build a reasonable sized betting bank and that will give you time to read Section 2 of Horse Race betting – How to make it pay where I will suggest ways that you can approach your horse race betting and turn it in to a profitable sideline or business as opposed to an expensive hobby.

Section 2

"Now we learn to fish"

Chapter 1

Knowledge is King

There is a story about the famous South African golfer Gary Player and I do not know if it is true or not but it does highlight an important fact about betting on horse races. Apparently after playing a particularly great shot someone said to him,

"Hey Gary, that was a lucky shot."

and apparently Player turned to the fan and said

"Yes, and its funny but the more I practice the luckier I get."

Sadly horse race betting is not like that. Placing more bets, either real or imaginary will not make you a better punter. The reason for this is simple; if you are losing money now and continue to approach your betting in the same manner you will continue to lose money.

There is an old adage, which goes something like, "In the land of the blind, the one eyed man is king." When it comes to horse race betting I would change that to "In the land of the uninformed, the knowledgeable man is king". What I mean by uninformed is a person who has not taken the trouble to learn the basics of horse racing and betting. H]The basics are the ability to read and understand form, know the effects of going, distance and weight on the potential outcome of any horse race. Possibly even more important, the knowledgeable punter knows which horse races they should avoid and which ones to have a bet on.

Hopefully not only will this book help to increase your understanding of how to bet successfully but also will point you in the right direction to further improve your judgment and knowledge. However, knowledge on its own is not enough, we have all met knowledgeable people who unfortunately do not have one ounce of common sense. So to be a successful punter you not only need to have the knowledge but also the judgment to know how and when to use that knowledge.

There are many different types of punter and I have come of with my own classification of ten different types. Before we go any further I would like you to take the time to study the 10 definitions and decide which best describes your present approach to betting on horse racing. This will be your starting point and hopefully by the time you have finished this book and applied its lessons you will be at number 10 and amongst the

5% of punters who make money from their horse race betting.

The 10 Types of Punter.

1. They back a horse because they like its name or because they always back grey horses in a race because they are easier to spot when watching the race on the TV.

2. These back the horse because a bloke in the betting shop has a cousin who knows a bloke who knows another bloke who works in the stable and says the horse is a cert.

3. This type back a horse because my favourite newspaper pundit has tipped it.

4. The fourth group back the horse because it is favourite so it must stand the best chance of winning.

5. These punters back the horse because they have read the comments in the Racing Post and based their selection on them.

6. Are "follow the crowd" punters who back when they see that a horse's price is dropping like a stone so believe that those in the know must think it is a good thing.

7. These punters back the horse because having looked at the form in the past it has done well on the same going or over the same distance.

8. Will only back a horse when they have studied the horse's form and looked at the trainer and jockeys current strike rate.

9. Will only back a horse when they see that on its past form on the type of track it is running on today hit looks a good bet. I have also checked the trainer and jockeys records at this track.

10. I have backed this horse because having   studied the whole field my selection looks well in. There are few if any negatives with regard to the course, distance and going and I have checked on the trainers and jockeys

current and course records and the evidence persuades me that my selection stands a very good chance of winning.

I suspect that if you are honest you will recognize yourself somewhere between number 1 and 7. Hopefully because you have had the sense to read this book you will be no lower than number 5. Even if you fall into the 1 to 4 bracket by following the guidelines in this book you will be able to turn your loses into profits.

Knowledge maybe the number one key that can help you make money backing horses but there is another factor, which is also important. Have you ever considered why bookmakers are so successful and profitable? For a start the odds they offer are slanted towards making them a profit whichever horse wins the race. This is called having an over round book and they will make anything from 7% upwards profit on turnover and for some races this profit can be considerably greater. It is possible for bookmakers too lose money especially if a heavily backed favourite wins but they come out on top more often than not.

Like any other business bookmakers have their overheads, the costs of running high street shops or having a pitch on a top race course are not cheap. To pay for this and to make a decent profit for the owner or investors requires the use of the very latest technology and business methods and expertise. The days of the corner street bookie are almost gone and the industry now is run mainly by multi million pound companies who employ accountants, strategists, marketers, and many other specialists whose ultimate job is to ensure that the pound or even "tenner" in your pocket ends up in their hands.

So what chance does the average punter stand against such high powered expertise? For most the answer is "not a lot" but it does not have to be like that. In simple terms the bookie wants your money and you want the bookies money. He approaches the job in a business like manner and if you treat your betting in a causal or carefree way there is only going to be one winner in the long term. However, if you adopt a professional and businesslike approach to your betting you will be starting to tilt the odds in your favour.

Try this little test to see if you have a business like approach:

1. How much did you win or lose betting on horse racing last month?

2. What factor effects how much you will place on one bet?

3. Do you keep a detailed record of each of your bets?

4. Do you have a specific betting bank or do you just use your everyday cash?

5. Do you know in which races you have the greatest success with, flat, hurdle, chases or all weather?

How did you do?

1. To be a successful punter you need a yardstick to measure success. The obvious measure is cash, how much you are making or losing. Many punters I know are secretly afraid of keeping this type of record because if they actually checked how much they gave the bookie each month it would put them off for ever. However, if you are going to be a successful punter you need this information at your fingertips.

2. Are you the type of person who puts a set amount on each bet or does the amount vary

according to outside factors such as how much you have in your pocket. Alternatively are you the type of punter who chases his or her loses and increases the stake after a losing bet in an attempt to recover the loss? The majority of successful punters have either a policy of level stakes or waging a percentage of their betting bank.

3. Do you know what bets you had last month? How much did you stake and how much did you win? This is the sort of information you need to know if you are serious about wanting to profit from your betting.

4. If you had a business you would almost certainly have a separate business bank account. If you are serious about making profits from racing then you should set aside an amount for your betting activities. It does not necessarily have to be put into an actual bank account but you should set it aside and use it for no other purpose than your gambling activities.

5. If you keep a record of all your bets this should also include details of the types of race involved. You may be surprised to find that you are more successful when you back

in hurdle races than chases or it could be the other way round. Perhaps you have more winners in maiden races rather than handicaps. Whatever your records show it could be an indicator of areas you should concentrate your horse race betting on.

In this first chapter I am concentrating on two important factors that you need to understand if you are to increase your chances of coming out ahead of the bookies. Knowledge and a business like or professional approach to what until now you may have just considered a hobby.

What are the steps that you can take today?

Read everything that you can about horse racing. There are literally hundreds of books out there on the subject; some are really good and informative whilst others are just a waste of paper. Unfortunately you may not discover which is which until you start to read them. I am going to list a few books that I have found useful over the years. Although some of them may be out of print by now the information is still good and you should be able to get a second hand copy from either Amazon or eBay.

1. Betting for as Living by Nick Mordin.

My copy of this book was printed in 1992 but is full of good information. It was written before the introduction of online betting and Exchange betting but it is still very much a good read for anyone who wants to increase their knowledge of racehorse betting. Published by Aesculus Press.

2. The Punters Friend-A guide to Racing and Betting –Jack Waterman

Originally published in 1987 my copy is an updated 2005 version. This book will be of interest to both the novice and the regular punter. It demystifies the world of horse racing and betting. Published by Virgin Books.

3. The Definitive Guide to Horse Race Betting – Edited by Nick Pulford

This book consists of excellent articles by some of the Racing Posts leading experts including Tom Segal (Pricewise). The latest edition is available from Amazon and is strongly recommended. Published by Racing Post.

Treat your betting as a business

To become more business like you should consider setting aside an amount to use as a betting bank. If you have followed the method outlined in Section One you should soon have a sizeable betting bank. But if for any reason you have decided not to adopt this approach you will still need to set aside money as a "betting bank". This does not have to be a huge amount but I would suggest you consider a sum that would be large enough for at least 20 bets using you usual stake. For example if your normal win bet is £1 then you should set a bank of £20 and if you usually bet £10 then you should set aside £200. This works on the fact that unless you are extremely unlucky or a real bad punter you should not have 20 successive losing bets. Staking plans and the amount you should place on each wager is discussed later in this book.

You also need some sort of book or file to keep your betting records in. It does not need to be anything grand or complicated. Fortunately the taxman does not regard winnings from gambling as taxable so these records are only going to be for your use.

A simple note of the date, horse, type of race, amount staked and details of the returns or lose and the resultant state of your betting bank is all that you need.

We have covered quite a bit of ground in this chapter and I hope given you something to think about. In Chapter Two we are going to move on to another important factor that you need to understand before we can move on to the nuts and bolts of horse race betting and that is your mindset.

Chapter 2

The Correct Mindset

I remember the very first bet I ever made on a horse race. It was the 1960 Derby and that will give you some idea of how old I really am. It would be another year before Betting Offices (or shops) would be legalised and put the old bookies runners out of business. Along with some of the other lads at work I looked at the list of runners in the paper and placed a bet of one shilling (5p for you young whiper snappers) on St Paddy. I have no idea why I picked that horse, maybe I had read something in the paper but anyway my shilling went on Lester Piggot's mount. Surprisingly it won at I think 7/1 and from then on I was hooked.

For the next few years I regularly handed a fair percentage of my wages across the counter to the bookies. Thankfully as time rolled on I acquired responsibilities such as a wife and a mortgage and combined with greater demands at work I rather put horse race betting to one side. I would have a flutter on the Grand National or The Derby, very rarely winning, but that was all. Then about twenty years ago I came across a book called "Braddock's Complete Guide to Horse Race Selection and Betting" by Peter Braddock. It was quite an eye opener and for the first time I realized that there was more to race horse betting than just a quick glance at the racing page and picking a selection. The book was originally published in 1983 and the latest edition I could find came out in 2004. Although a bit dated now much of the content is as relevant today as when it was written. It is well worth the read.

Having read Braddock's book I started dipping into the betting market again. Not in a big way but I did have an idea that I could see betting as a way of supplementing my fast approaching pension. Not surprisingly I had some successes but even more failures and my betting bank was diminishing at an alarming rate.

By then I had also started building up a comprehensive library of horse racing and betting books and my level of knowledge was growing. However, there definitely seemed to be something I was missing, how was it a few people seemed to be able to make regular profits from horse race betting whilst the rest of us could not get close to breaking even. It was around this time that I read a self-development books by one of those American" gurus on "How to realize your full potential". One of the sections of the book was about mindset and how to be a success you must have the right mindset. I did not fancy his suggestion that I should "walk over hot coals" to discover myself but the concept of mindset intrigued me. I started to wonder if this also applied to punters and the more I researched into it the more certain I became that to make regular profits from betting you really did need the right mindset.

O.K. but what is "Mindset"

Basically your mindset is the manner in which you deal with the successes, failures and setbacks that every punter encounters on a regular basis. It can be said to be the interface between winning or losing and your reaction to that. For example whilst one person's mindset will allow them to view a loss philosophically another person might rant, rage and blame everyone except him or herself.

Surely no one enjoys losing a bet? Of course not but it is the way that one reacts to such a setback that can define how likely it is that you can make consistent profits from your betting campaign. Possibly it was Kipling, in his poem "If" who summed it up best:

"If you can meet with Triumph and Disaster and treat those two impostors just the same; Then you are a man, my boy"

"If" Rudyard Kipling

If you ever go into a betting shop it is always interesting to see how people react when their bet loses. I have noticed about five different types of reaction:

- "That jockey couldn't ride a clothes horse, he was rubbish."

- "What a swindle, it's all fixed anyway"

- "I was going to back that winner but I got a hot tip for the second"

- "I'm not surprised, I couldn't pick the winner in a walk over"

- "If I double up on my next bet I get my losses back"

In the first two cases the punter is ready to blame anyone but himself, the third doesn't trust his own judgment, the fourth is a fatalist who does not expect to win so will almost certainly be proved right and the final guy is a fully paid up member of the "fool and his money" club and a ready contributor to the bookmakers Caribbean holiday fund.

If you seriously want to make your horse race betting pay you need to develop a winning mindset. This means you must do the following:

1. Accept responsibility for your actions.

2. Accept that there will be losing bets.

3. Learn from your mistakes

4. Never miss an opportunity to increase your knowledge.

5. Accept betting for you is a business not a hobby.

6. Take the long-term view.

1. Accept responsibility for your actions.

It is very easy to blame someone else for your mistakes. It was the trainer, jockey, the going, distance or any one of a dozen other things. What you are really saying is that you missed something when you assessed the race. You just did not notice the trainers long losing run or the fact that the jockey has never won on this course. How come it slipped past you that the horse had never raced over the distance or on today's going before? So rule number one in building a winning mindset is NEVER BLAME ANYONE ELSE WHEN **YOU** GET IT WRONG.

2. Accept there will be losing bets.

If you expect every bet to win you are going to be sadly disappointed. In fact if you back horses in the 3/1 to 5/1 price range and have a 30% to 40% success rate this will be enough to show you a steady profit. Losing is just as much a part of horse race betting as winning and you have to accept this. In any form of gambling there is an element of risk and if you are into horse race betting for the long term you need to keep your mind focused on the amount of risk or liability your bet could incur. For instance, if you use level stakes of say 5% for each of your bets then a loss or even a series of losses will not be bank breaking. Risk half your bank on one bet and a loss would be a catastrophe. It is important to consider in your mind the potential effect of a loss as well as the gains should it win.

3. Learn from your mistakes.

Once a race is over and the result known the average punter loses all interest and moves on to the next race. This is not they way of the serious player who will go back to the formbook, study how the race was run and possibly watch a recording to see what if anything they missed in assessing the race. Ask yourself, why did a horse I thought had a very good chance of winning the race not do so. It may be simply that the horse had some bad luck in running but there again could this have been foreseen? For instance the formbook might tell you that the horse you fancied was usually slow from the stalls but could come like a train towards the end of a race. This might be all right in small fields but there could be problems if there are 20 or more runners in a five-furlong sprint. Again perhaps you missed something in the form of the winner that could have affected your choice. The truth is that you will learn more from the bets you lose than from the ones you win. Remember the old saying,

"The man who never made a mistake never made anything".

4. Never Miss an Opportunity to increase your knowledge

There are hundreds of books on the subject of horse racing and betting. Some are very good, some not so good and others written by authors who really have very little to say that is relevant. Never the less as your knowledge grows you will soon be able to sort the gemstones from the lumps of coal. I have quite a large library of racing books that I have built up over the years. Although I have bought some brand new many came second hand either from Amazon, eBay or local car boot sales.

Knowledge does not have to be expensive and as many of the best books are out of print buying second hand off the Internet is the best way obtain some of the books. Most people connected with horse racing subscribe to *The Racing Post* the industries daily newspaper. It currently costs around £60 a month for the paper copy but you can subscribe to the online edition for £14.50 a month and I find that quite adequate for my needs. As well as the race cards and form sections for each of the day's race meeting the paper also has the latest racing news and articles. Early in both the flat and National Hunt season there are informative articles about some of the top stables and their hopes for the coming season. These can prove both informative and profitable.

As well as books and newspapers there are videos available on horse racing and betting which can be worth watching. At one time I used to be a great fan of the Channel 4 Saturday Morning racing program "The Morning Line" but I am beginning to believe it has lost its way a bit over the last couple of years. Not as good as it was but even so there can be the odd tidbit worth picking up from the show.

I don't know whether it is advancing age or just that we all suffer from information overload but it seems to be getting harder to retain so many facts. Therefore I have taken to jotting down interesting tit bits in a notebook. For instance a trainer being interviewed on TV before a race the other day said he thought the ground was to soft for his runner but we could expect a different performance when it got good ground. That got jotted down in the notebook, and this will just be another factor to consider when that horse next runs.

5. Accept that Betting, for you, is a business and not a hobby

Why do you bet on horses? Is it for the fun or excitement, is it the thought of making a quick killing and loads of cash quickly. If you answered yes to either of these questions that it's fine but this book is not for you. This book is for people who want to make a good first or second long-term income by betting on the outcome of horse races. If you come into this second group then you need to accept the fact that you are running a business and the only way you can measure your business success is by the profit you make. The joy of your business is that once you have set aside a bank your overheads are low, your profits tax-free and your prospects are good. Do not try and make a £1000 profit in your first week, especially if you are starting with a £100 bank!! Slow and steady progress will reap its reward. I have already mentioned the need to keep records so that you can monitor your progress.

6. Take the long-term view

There will be days when you will not make a profit, there may well be losing weeks or even the odd month but that is not what is important. The important figure is how much you have made over the year. Greed and or impatience are two factors that could ruin your chances of making horse race betting pay. Guard against them, At first your bank might appear to be growing at a very slow rate but in time if you are using a percentage of your bank staking method (which is discussed elsewhere in this book) it will hopefully grow at a much faster rate in the months to come.

Chapter 3

Show me the money

Your Betting Bank

If you are serious about making your horse race betting pay and provide you with a useful income you need to start thinking about the money. The first decision you will have to make is how large a betting bank you are going to have. Your betting bank is the amount of money that you are going to set aside to use purely for the purpose of betting on racehorses. It needs to be two things:

1. An amount of money, that you could in the worst case afford to lose without it causing you severe financial distress.

2. An amount of money that you are prepared to leave in your betting bank for a reasonable amount of time without making any withdrawals.

If you have used the information in Section 1 there should be no problem in building an adequate betting bank.

It is very important that you keep your betting bank completely separate from your other money and never use the cash in your betting bank for any other purpose until the bank reaches a pre planned level. As part of your planning it is a good idea to decide how large you want your betting bank to grow before withdrawing any of the money. For instance you may decide that you want to grow your betting bank until it reaches a certain figure. Once it has passed this level you may wish to draw some money from it for your own use. For example if you start with a betting bank of £200 you might want to build it up to £1000. Once it has passed this sum you could decide to withdraw the excess for your own personal use. If you remember from the chapter on Mindset one of the important factors was that you are in this for the long term. Unlike the average losing punter you should not be looking for instant gratification, with one big win but a steady growth in your betting bank.

How much money you can make also depends on two factors:

1. The amount of money in your betting bank.

2. The percentage of successful bets that you have.

1. The amount of money that you have in your betting bank

Only you can decide how large your betting bank should be. It does not matter if you start with a betting bank of £20 or £2000 you can apply the principles outlined in this book to grow your bank at a steady rate. One option is to spend a couple of months putting money aside towards your betting bank while at the same time running a paper trial to get some experience of being a *wise punter.* This should also give you more confidence for when you do start using your actual betting bank.

During any paper trial it is just as important to keep a record of these transactions, as they will provide you with some important information that will be useful when you start playing for real. Imagine that your starting bank is £1000. The points that you should note are:

1. The Number of "paper" bets you made during the trial.

2. The number of winners and their prices.

3. The longest losing run.

4. How much would you have won or lost if you had backed your selection at level odds. i.e. 5% of the bank (£50 a bet). Also how much would you have won or lost betting 5% of the actual bank. (i.e. if the bank had risen to £1100 a bet of £55 and if it had dropped to £950 a bet of £47.50)

This is the kind of information you will be keeping and reviewing regularly once you start betting in earnest.

Money Management

Behind any successful business you will find an accountant, or in many cases teams of accountants carefully monitoring the financial state of the business. Well guess what; in your horse race betting business you are going to have to be your own accountant. The success or failure of your venture into horse race betting is going to be almost as dependent upon how well you manage the money side of your business as how good your horse selections are.

 Your first important decision as "Bookie Basher Limited" is to set the amount of your betting bank. After this some kind of simple business plan with profit projections would be useful. But how can you make financial projections in such a precarious business as backing horses?

Admittedly forecasting is not a precise art but after your paper trial you have some useful information at your fingertips that can help you. First of all you know how many trial bets you had and the success rate. For example lets say that you had 20 bets and they produced 5 winners.

Your win rate is 25%

The prices of the winning horses were 5/1. 4/1 3/1 and 2 at 2/1

The average price of your winners was 3.2/1

Your longest losing run 5 races

Your longest winning run was 2

The actual sequence was:

L L 3/1 L L L 5/1 L L 2/1 4/1 L L L L L L 2/1 L L

Had you backed at a 5% level stake of your starter bank the result would have been:

£1000,£950,£900,£1050,£1000,£950,£900,£11150,£1100£1050,£1150,£1350,£1300,£1250,£1200,£1150,£1250,
£1200,£1150.

That would shown a profit of £150 or 15% of the bank

Had you backed at 5% of the actual bank at the time of the bet the figures would have been:

£1000,£950,£902.,£1037,£985,£935,£1169,£1111,£1055£1108,£1329,£1262,£1199,£1139,£1082,£1027,£1129,

£1072,£1018.

That would have shown a profit of just £18 or 1.8% of the bank. The figures in the second example of been rounded up or down to the nearest pound for simplicities sake.

This example is not designed to show that level stakes are better than using the percentage of actual bank they simply show that results can vary. Which of the two methods is better is dependent upon several factors if for instance you can achieve 40% wins at an average price of 4/1 then the second method would prove more profitable.

The main point of this exercise is to prove that the only way you can make fact based decisions on what is the most profitable staking system for you is by keeping good records of your betting activity.

As your knowledge grows you will come across many different types of staking plans. I remember in my younger days there used to be a weekly racing newspaper that was published on Saturdays. Every week there was a full-page advert for a racing service that claimed to give a winner everyday. What was impressive was it named each day's winner and the prices for the previous month to prove the claim. You could purchase a week's selections that the advert said would be posted to you sometime during the previous week.

Having sent off my money, not an inconsiderable portion of my weekly wage I sat back and waited for the names of the promised winners to drop through the letterbox. What I actually got was a list of runners for each and every race each with a rating beside their name. What you had to do was back the top rated horse in the first race and if that lost double up your stake in the next and continue to do this until you got a winner. Needless to say I did not get very far with it but it was a lesson learnt.

This type of staking system is known as the Martingale System. It can come in many guises and is often favoured by producers of commercial racing systems who make exaggerated claims for their products. Doubling up your stake after every loser is basically a fast track to the poor house. If your original bet is £1 and you have a losing run of 10 bets then your stake to try and win that £1 back will be £512! The advice is to avoid this staking method or any derivative of the Martingale System.

Another Staking System that you may come across if called the Fibonacci Staking Plan. It is not dissimilar to the Martingale in that you have to increase your stake following a losing bet however it is not quite such a straightforward progression. If your first bet loses you bet the same stake on your next selection but after this the progressive staking fires up. The required stake is then calculated by adding the value of the previous two bets so after 2 losers the stake will have been 1 + 1 = 2 so If you started with £1 and the first 2 bets were losers the stake on the third bet would be £2. This progression would continue until you found a winner.

$$1+1+2+3+5+8+13+21+34+55+89+144$$

Using the Fibonacci Staking Plan is another that will quickly decimate your bank after a relatively short losing run. Definitely another method of staking that is best avoided.

There are a variety of other staking methods such as Barry Hughes Retirement Plan and La Bouchere which both have points to recommend them. I do not use them as I prefer the level stakes approach but if you are interested you can find out more about both these staking plans by searching for them on the Internet.

There is one draw back with the level stakes approach and that is it takes a considerable time to build your bank. Using the percentage of your actual bank also presents some problems because the calculations will produce some strange amounts and it is difficult to place a bet of say £5.67 or £7.83 although this would be quite acceptable if your were betting with Betfair. Personally I would round up or down to the nearest whole pound.

My solution is to bet level stakes and if I go below my original bank I keep at that. However, Once my bank has grown by 20% I increase my stake by that percentage, so in this case if I had been staking £5 I would then increase it to £6 and keep it there unless the bank dropped down to its starting level when I would revert to the original stake. Each time the bank increases by a further 20% I would increase the stake level. This way when you have doubled your bank you will have also doubled your stake. This seems to me a good compromise.

Another factor to consider is the price of the horses you are prepared to back. I am assuming that you are wise enough to realize that backing any horse that is odds on is no way to make money. You will make more money backing one 4/1 winner than you will from backing four odds on winners. Obviously there are other factors besides price that will determine whether you back a selection but personally I prefer to back horses that are priced between 4/1 and 8/1. In later chapters we shall be looking at the various other selection criteria but no matter how confident I felt about a horses chances I would be wary of backing those priced below 3/1.

We have spent the first three chapters of this section of Horse Race Betting –How to Make It Pay talking not about horses, form, going or any of the other aspects of picking winners. What we have done is talk about YOU and your attitude and knowledge. To go from hobby punter to a serious player means a change of mindset and attitude.

Horse racing is a thrilling and exciting sport and it is difficult not to get emotionally involved in that excitement. We all have favourite horses we love to see run and win, there are jockeys and trainers who we hold in high regard. However, when it comes to finding winners we must suppress emotion and simply evaluate the facts (form) and what ever you do ignore the "good thing" that comes from a friend of a friend whose cousin works in a racing stable.

Most peoples image of a professional gambler is a somewhat larger than life character in a loud checked suit. These days they are likely to be quiet serious individuals who spend far more time on their computers than they do at the races. This may not be as exciting as standing in the Silver Ring or being at the bookies watching your selection charge up the final furlong but it will almost certainly be more profitable in the long term.

The question is which do you really want, excitement or profit?

Chapter 4

The Tools for the Job.

At this point you will have hopefully be convinced of the need to add to your knowledge of horse racing and betting. You can do this by reading books by experts and possibly watching some video tutorials. You now understand the importance of mindset and are full of enthusiasm to get started to make your horse race betting pay a good return for your time and effort. You have also calculated how much you can afford to set aside as a betting bank so in other words it is all systems go.

Opening an account with a bookmaker

However, there are a few other items that have to be put in place before you can start making money. First of all you will almost certainly need a betting account with a bookmaker. You can of course simply go round to your local betting shop to place your bets but not only can that be inconvenient you can also be tempted to stop and watch a couple of races and to make a coupled of impulse bets. If you have used the bank building system in Section One you will have quite a few online accounts with book makers as well as a Betfair Betting Exchange account.

If you have not followed the bank building system you may have to open an online account with a bookmaker. To do this you will need to pay a deposit, as there is no credit betting allowed. A deposit can be as little as £10 but I would opt to open 5 separate accounts using 20% of your bank to open each account. Before you open any online bookmakers account I would advise you to thoroughly reread Section 1 of this book before opening any online betting account.

Because the competition for your business is so fierce most online bookmakers will offer incentives for you to open your account with them. If you visit www.top100bookmakers.com/signup.php you will not only get links to the top 100 bookmaking sites but will be able to see what bonuses each is offering and the minimum amount that you need to deposit to open an account.

The one thing bookmakers do not like is a regular winner so you should be aware that there is always a risk that if you become too successful your account may be closed down. Bookies are not good losers but fortunately there are so many online bookmakers these days that this should not be a problem. Fortunately, even if you became incredibly lucky and become wealthy by taking all the bookmakers to the cleaners the betting exchanges will still welcome you with open arms. Betfair and the other betting exchanges do not care if you win or lose they will still get their commission.

The Racing Post

Nearly every national morning newspaper includes a section on horse racing and includes details of the day's race cards but they vary a great deal in the quality and information they provide. If you are serious about making money from horse race betting you ideally need access to a daily copy of The Racing Post. By access I do not mean reading the pages posted on the betting shop wall (although this is better than nothing). The only problem, especially when you are starting out, is the cost. There are two options, you an either subscribe to the newspaper or the online edition. At the time of writing it costs around £2 a day for the printed edition but you can visit www.racingpost.co.uk and visit the race card pages and news page for free but for the serious punter you would really need a subscription to the Racing Post Membership Club. There are two levels of subscription. The "Essential" level costs £14.50 a month and the Ultimate will set you back £26 per month.

Both levels of membership will give you access to: Information, Horse Tracking and Racing UK video Replays.

In Addition Ultimate level gives members additionally:

Unlimited At The Races Video Replays, Unlimited Racing UK Replays, Pricewise Paper Tips, Pricewise Extra, The Extra Edge and Daily Video Tips.

Whether you opt for the paper edition or one of the two on line subscription offers is a matter of personal choice. If you do not intend to bet everyday and perhaps because of work commitments or other reasons buy the paper on the days you bet will be the cheapest option. If on the other hand you are going to bet regularly the subscriptions may be a better option. In my case I take the Racing Post everyday except Sundays. (I cannot abide Sunday racing, the quality of the runners is poor and for some reason form seems to go out of the window.)

My main reason for going for the paper copy is a section called "Signposts". As the title suggests this gives signposts to relevant data on the days racing. The Hot Trainer table lists the trainers with the best win-run percentages in the last 14 days; it also gives those with then worst percentage in the Cold Trainers list. There is a list giving the best and worst trainers percentages for that particular course. There is a similar lists of the best and worse performing jockeys, jockeys who have only one mount at the meeting, something that at times can be significant and details of horses that have traveled long distances to the meeting. Usually if a Southern trainer sends one horse all the way to a small meeting at a Northern or Scottish track this might indicate he considers it has a real chance. Although I have known such plans come unstuck before now so there is no guarantee it is always worth noting. There are also much more data that can help you either making or rejecting a selection.

My other reason for preferring the print edition is because I can scribble notes all over the race cards as I work out my selections. Or perhaps the truth is that I am a dinosaur who prefers the printed page to the computer screen.

If you do not wish to spend money on subscriptions there is a way that you can access much of the Racing Post information for free. You will need to open an account with the Paddy Power online betting service. If you follow the advice in Section 1 this will be no doubt one of the companies you will have opened an account with. Once you have an account simply go to:

www.paddypower.com/racing/horse-racing

Select the race you are interested in and click the Green "Tips" Tab. You can then see:

> The Selection Box which has the selections for that race from Newmarket, Postdata, Spotlight, The North, RP Ratings, Topspeed and Lambourne..

Moving down any "Steamers" for the race are shown, followed by "Hot" and "Cold" jockey statistics and the same information regarding trainers Finally you have details of 7 Day winners, horses that have traveled and horses running for the first time for a new trainer

At The Races web site

Another web site that is full of good information is www.attheraces.com, which also has much of the same information as the Racing Post site. Amongst the information available on the site are:

News, The Days Race Cards, Results Service, Tips, Stable Tours, Race Replays, Speed Ratings and Market Movers.

Recently they have introduced a further service, which enables you to printout the Race card, Form details and Time Form ratings. The real bonus at the moment is that access to this site is totally free. All you have to do is register online and you can access all areas of the site.

Both The Racing Post (RP) and the At The Races (ATR) sites have a great deal to recommend them but possibly because it is free I tend to use the ATR site combined with my copy of the RP to do my research. It is also worth remembering the information that can be gleaned from Paddy Power's web site.

What I do find a little surprising is the fact that despite there being far more information and facilities available to the punter today compared to when I first started betting their success rate seems no better. Those of you who can remember the early days of the Betting Offices will remember the small smoke filled rooms. A list of runners would be hung on the wall and a "Boardman" would chalk up the odds as they came over the tannoy. When a race was in progress you also had to rely on the tannoy commentary to find out how your runner was doing. Nowadays betting shop are far more comfortable places with wall-to-wall televisions to show all the action and the odds.

Today it is perfectly possible to be a professional horse race punter without ever going near a racecourse or betting shop. A few years ago that would not have been possible but now thanks to online betting and a comprehensive TV coverage of horse racing it is not only possible but also quite common. It is at least a couple of years since I last went a race meeting and I rarely go into my local betting shop.

Again in the "dark days" televised racing, was only featured on Saturday afternoons or for special races such as The Derby or Grand National. This was very much the preserve of BBC and ITV. Both more or less abandoned the sport and left Channel 4 as the only terrestrial channel with any real presence although in the last few days ITV has out bid Channel 4 for racing coverage for the next few years. However, today the gap in racing coverage has been filled by two satellite services, At The Races and Racing UK. Between them they cover nearly every race in the UK and Ireland as well as some French Racing and the Major Dubai Racing Festival.

At the Races is on Sky Channel 415 Virgin 534 and Racing UK is Sky 432 Virgin 536. At The Races comes, as part of the package for most subscribers to Sky or Virgin but there is a subscription charge of £20 a month for Racing UK. As well as being able to view the races in real time it is also possible to watch a rerun later. I find it is amazing what you miss at the first time of watching. I have one of those Tivo boxes, which allows up to 500 hours of recording so I can keep the previous 30 days racing to review at any time.

As I mentioned earlier if you take out a subscription to the Racing Posts "Ultimate" service this includes access to both At The Races and Racing UK's replay service which may be the best way if you are not able to watch live because of other commitments.

I have to give one word of warning when it comes to watching any racing on TV. You should be looking for potential and pointers to store away for the future. However, there is always the temptation to leap in and place a bet on a horse that you suddenly fancy or one that a pundit has just highlighted. For this reason I always like to place my bets before racing starts for the day and then switch off my computer. As I bet purely online these days the thought of having to go and switch on the machine, call up the web page and actually place a bet is enough to deter me. It may be a form of laziness but I have been grateful to it on many occasions.

If you want to make your Horse Race Betting Pay then the only bets you should make should be on horses that you have thoroughly researched and rated against their opposition. I am sorry to say that there will be a day when having selected a horse in just one race at a meeting it will lose while several of your considered but unbacked selections will win. It will happen, and has to me on many occasions and it is a real test of your mindset. On the plus side there have been more days when my bet has won but most if not all of my considered but unbacked fancies have lost their races.

Timeform

Finally I should mention TimeForm Publications. The well-known gambler Phil Bull founded it in 1948. Bull believed that it was possible to establish a mathematical link to a horse's performance based on the time a horse recorded in a race.

According to the publishers, a Timeform rating represents "the merit of the horse expressed in pounds and is arrived at by careful examination of its running against other horses using a scale of weight for distance beaten which ranges from around 3 lb. a length at five furlongs and 2 lb. a length at a mile and a quarter to 1 lb. a length at two miles.

The race-by-race ratings are interesting and like any rating system they have good and bad days. I still maintain that you should do your own thorough study of form and make your selection based on what you think and not someone else's ideas.

In 2006 Betfair purchased Timeform Publications and since then the race-by-race Timeform ratings have been freely available on several web sites including www.attheraces.co.uk and www.betfair.com. At the beginning of each Flat and Jump Racing season Timeform bring out at their "50 To Follow" book for about £10 which is worth studying.

Chapter 5

Getting Down to Business

There are two things in our lives today that many of us do not have enough of and they are time and money. If you are to become a successful punter you will have to make better use of both.

Time

For the majority of us, two events take up the largest portions of our time, work and sleep. Reducing either is not going to benefit either finances or welfare. This still leaves the problem that to become a serious and successful punter you will need to find the time to spend pursuing your objective of making money from betting. It may mean spending less time watching television, socialising with friends or spending time on other interests but the rewards can be worth it. Before you go any further you should decide if you are prepared to devote a reasonable amount of time to the business of horse race betting. Hopefully the answer will be yes.

The next step is to decide how much time you can devote to studying the race cards and increasing your knowledge of the sport of kings. It may be only an hour a day or longer. Perhaps you are so busy you can only make time at the weekends. What ever your situation it is important that once you decide upon a realistic amount of time available that you stick to it.

The available amount of time will also affect the number of races you can reasonably be expected to review. If you only have one hour a day you will not be able to go through all the days' meetings and study every race too any depth. This in itself is no real problem because no one should expect to be able to select a winner from every race. The secret is to select the right racers to spend your time studying.

Some of the most successful professional punters tend to specialise in specific types of races. These could be only Flat Races, National Hunt or All Weather and even these can be broken down further. There are professional gamblers who concentrate on 2-year-old races whilst others might specialise in long distance flat races.

Money

If we are honest we all have some element of greed in our make up. Who has not dreamt at some time of winning the lottery or getting rich in some other way? There is nothing wrong in that but greed can ruin your chances of making a regular income through horse race betting. There is nothing wrong in wishing to be better off but when it comes to horse racing it is important to have realistic expectations. You can make money but forget those exaggerated claims some system sellers promise. Recently I read one, which claimed you could turn £100 into £30000 in 6 months. Forget it, it will not happen!! Profits will come slowly at first but increase as your bank and experience grow.

The reason that 95% of punters lose when betting is because they think it is an easy way to make money. It is not unless, of course, you are a bookie.

Having got that out of the way let us get started.

You have set aside one hour a day to study the days racing and you have got the days race card either open in front of you or on your computer screen.

There are quite a few types of horse race that it is best to avoid.

The Big Saturday Race.

On most Saturdays in the UK you will find that the major horse race will be a handicap event with a big prize for the winning connections. These races invariably attract a good-sized field and are the main races that the horse racing journalists and tipsters concentrate on. It is not an accident that most of these races are sponsored by major high street bookies because they are the most profitable types of race for them. In any handicap race it can be difficult to find the winner but with large fields and quality horses it can be even harder. This type of race is good to watch but not such a good betting proposition.

Large Field Sprints.

A sprint races over 5 or 6 furlongs especially the more valuable ones attract large fields and can present the punter with real problems. Firstly how well a horse runs may depend more on the draw rather than known form. Horses drawn close to the inner running rail may have a distinct advantage over another horse drawn on the outside of the field. An additional problem is that no matter how good a horse is, if it does not get out of the stalls promptly it may lose its chance of winning before the race has gone a furlong. Also if the horse is a known fast finisher it can easily find its path blocked by slower horses near the finish. Large field sprints are definitely races to avoid. Conversely there are punters who specialise in sprint races but even they tend to avoid those with big 20 runner plus fields.

Apprentice and amateur jockey's races.

Generally the standard of riding and jockeyship has improved considerably over the last few decades but there is no substitute for experience. Young jockeys and those who do not race ride on a regular basis are always liable to make mistakes and misjudgements during a race. These again are races to watch a see if you can spot some future talent but not to bet on.

As a general rule the better the quality of the race the better a betting proposition it is. Horses in Group races (Group 1, 2 & 3 are the top level of flat racing) are more likely to run true to their form. At the lower levels Class 5 & 6 horse tend to be far more inconsistent and this is an additional factor to consider.

According to the rules of racing all the horses should be ridden to give them the very best chance of winning. However, in many races there are possibly only three or four horses that are actually running in the race to win. Some will be running purely to sharpen them up and improve their fitness for future races. There will also be others running for other reasons such as it is the horses owners local track and they like to see him run even if it has no chance of winning.

I always find it interesting when in the racing press or on television the trainer or pundit will say that such and such a horse has been "Laid Out" for a particular race. This means that the horse's training and recent runs have been aimed at getting it ready to give its very best for this specific race. Does this mean that in his previous races it was not tuned up to win?

Class

In the UK horseracing is like football in that it has it own leagues for teams of different abilities. Like football teams horses can go up or down a league dependant upon their ratings. It is always interesting to note when horses go up or down. A horse may have won several races in Class 4 but never win when raised up to Class 3 so this could be a guide when deciding to make it a selection or not.

Flat Racing

- Class 1 – Listed Handicaps of 96 -110+

- Class 2 - Handicaps of 86 -100, 91 – 105, 96 – 110, and Classified Stakes of 0 -95

- Class 3 – Handicaps of 76 – 90, 81 – 95, and Classified Stakes 0 -85, 0 – 90

- Class 4 – Handicaps of 66 – 80, 71 – 85

- Class 5 – Handicaps of 56 – 70, 61 – 75

- Class 6 – Handicaps of 46 -60, 51 – 65

- Class 7 Classified Stakes 0-45

National Hunt

- Class 1 – Pattern (Grade 1,2,& 3) and Listed Races

- Class 2 – Open Handicaps and Handicaps 0 – 140+

- Class 3 – Handicaps of 0-120, 0 – 135, and Novice Handicaps 0 -120, 0 – 135

- Class 4 – Handicaps of 0- -100, 0 -115, and Novice Handicaps 0 – 10 0, 0 – 115

- Class 5 – Handicaps of 0 -85, 0 -95 and Novice Handicaps of 0 -85, 0-95 and Classified Stakes 0 -85, 0 -95

- Class 6 - National Hunt Flat Races and Hunter Steeple Chases

I find it surprising that many punters seem to ignore the class of race a horse ran in previously. For instance would a horse, which came second in a class 3 race, be able to beat a horse that won its last class 4 race? The answer is quite possibly it might but if you only considered the fact that one horse was a winner last time out and the other only a runner up you might decide it unlikely.

Obvious Indicators

Knowing how to read and interoperate form is vital although it is not the intention of this book to go into the minutia of form stiudy. There are plenty of good books to help you try and master the art studying horse racing form. Although in all honesty nobody ever "masters" the subject. However to help you there is a list of recommended reading list at the back of the book. At first you may find it a little perplexing but with practice you will see the benefits of your new knowledge in terms of increased winning bets.

However, I do want to highlight some of the obvious indicators that surprisingly many punters seem to ignore.

The Going

I was once told that if the going is heavy look for horses with big feet because they were able to go through the mud better. I am not sure if this is true or not but it most certainly is true that the going (underfoot, or should it be under hoof) conditions can affect the outcome of a race. The majority of horses run well when the going is good, that is when there is a little "give" in the ground but there are some horses who perform far better when the going is either "firm" or in other cases "soft". When reading a horse's form note the going the last time it was ran well, that is it won or was placed. If they have performed well in the past on today's going that is a plus.

Distance

Most racehorses are bred to race over specific distances. This is particularly true of flat race horses. A sprinter may be at its best over 5 or 6 furlongs, a middle distance horse up to a mile and a half and anything beyond is considered a long distance race. Seven-furlong races are interesting because many sprinters find the extra furlong a little to far from them but the milers find it too short. As a result if you find a horse that has a good record over seven furlongs can be well worth following in such distance races.

The situation is slightly different with National Hunt horses that tend as youngsters (that is 5 to 6 year olds) to run in hurdle races of 2 or 2½ miles. Many National Hunt horses as they grow older progress to the bigger obstacles in chases which are normally run over distances of 3 miles plus. In flat races it is mainly about speed although stamina has to be considered in longer flat races but in National Hunt stamina can be a more important factor when searching for winners. This is particularly true when the going is classed as "heavy".

Finding Form Lines & Weight

You may find that some of the horses in the field will have raced each other before and it should be possible calculate how well they can be expected to perform again this time. There are some factors that may indicate that just because one horse beat another in one race that they will not beat them in this one. Firstly you need to compare the weight they carried before to the weight difference today. In addition to the weight allotted it is possible for a horse to be carrying a penalty of between 3 – 10 lb. for a win in its previous race. In many cases a trainer will counter this by giving the ride to an apprentice or conditional jockey who dependant upon the number of winners he or she has ridden may be able to claim up to 10lbs from the horse allotted weight.

If two horses have not raced against each other before it may be possible to find a form line by finding in their past form a horse they have both run against. Compare both there performances against this horse and it could give you an idea of who might come out on top today.

When studying form you should always give the most recent run the greatest weighting particularly if that run was within the previous 30 days. The older the form the less reliable it will be.

Value

Last but not least there is the concept of value. In simple terms you find value when you discover a horse that is priced at say 8/1 when you consider its true odds should be nearer 5/1. First of all you have to consider the factors that decide upon how the odds are calculated. The price of each runner in a race depends upon the weight of money that punters are prepared to wager on each horse. Normally this will be a fair reflection of a horse chances but there will be many occasions when the market gets it wrong and this provides an opportunity for the aware punter to profit.

Statistically favourites win around 33% of all races and that means that to break even all favourites would have to be priced at 2/1 but of course they are not.

The mathematics behind this is

100 Divided by 2 + 1 = 33%

Now a 5/1 chance has a 16.6% chance of winning

100   Divided by 5 + 1 = 16.6%

If that horse we looked at that was priced at 8/1 i.e. had an 11.11% chance of winning but we thought the true odd should have been 5/1 or 16.6% this would represent a value bet. By no means will all your "value" bets be successful but we are in the game for the long term and if your judgement is sound you are likely to get a couple of winners in 8 selections (25% success rate) and this will give you a fair profit something you will not make backing favourites.

The problem with value is that it is a very subjective judgement, but the more you search for it the better you will become at spotting the opportunities.

My Method

At this point I am going to tell you how I come up with my selections:

1. I look at the race cards and quickly eliminate those races that I always avoid which I mentioned early in the Chapter.

2. Next I dismiss any race where there are horses running for the first time. If you have horses with no form to assess how can you know what they are capable of?

3. Of the races that are left I start with the highest class or grade and look briefly at the form to see if I can see a possible selection. If there is I study the form more closely and eliminate any horse that I think stands no realistic chance of winning. Hopefully I will now have just 3 or 4 horses to study in detail. I look for form lines, check on both the trainers and jockeys current statistics to see if they are "hot" or "cold" and see what their records are on this particular course.

4. Having completed my study of the form the next consideration is the price of the horse I fancy. From experience I know that to make a decent profit from betting you only need to have a success rate of 25%, which is one winner out of every four selections and that is not an

impossible target. To profit with such a success rate requires you to only back selections priced at 3/1 or higher. In fact I rarely bet at odds of lower than 4/1 but there are occasionally exceptions when I have a very strong fancy for a horse as low as 3/1. The important point is to check that I am satisfied that I am getting value for my bet.

5. When I finished assessing my first race either having made a selection or discarding it I go to the next highest grade race and repeat the process. Dependant upon the time I have available and the number of selections I can find I will have between 1 and 3 bets a day. If I cannot find a suitable selection on any day I just leave it and wait for tomorrow. Never just place a bet on a horse because you think you have to bet everyday.

6. Finally no matter how strongly I fancy horse's chances I will always stick to my staking plan.

So there you are that in brief is how I do it, it's not exactly rocket science and finding 2 or 3 winners out of 10 selections should not be beyond anybody's capabilities.

Chapter 6

Other Considerations

In the last chapter I outlined the simple process I use to find my selections but to be honest there are other considerations that come into my reckoning that do not necessarily show in the formbook. Despite what you may have read in the novels of Dick Francis or John Francome British horseracing is one of the most honest and tightly controlled in the world. There is, I believe far less skulduggery or dishonesty in racing as there are in many other sports.

However, to believe that all the horses in every race are running to win is to be living in Never Never Land. There are many reasons why horses are entered into specific races and some of the reasons are:

- To win or be placed and get the prize money.
- To sharpen them up for a future race.

- Because the owner pays the training fees and likes to see the horse run occasionally.
- To get some form in order to get a handicap rating.
- Because one of the stables other horses is running at the meeting and it is just as cheap to send two horse in a horsebox to a meeting as one.

There are probably lots of other reasons that I have not thought of but you will get the idea. This might seem to make the job of finding winners even more difficult that it already is but this is not necessarily so. Simply by understanding trainers methods and habits can give you a big advantage over less informed punters.

There are around 600 licensed trainers in the UK and it would be impossible to study the methods of them all but knowledge of some trainers could prove profitable.

For instance I have a note of a trainer who has a high percentage of winners when he sends them over 150 miles away to run. Another who wins many races with horses that had just qualified for a handicap rating. There is another stable that is well known for having heavy bets on their horse when they strongly fancy one of their runners.

I have no special connection with any racing stable so how did I learn this information? The answer is that I listen to the "experts" who cover TV racing, particularly At The Races and Racing UK. It is not unusual for their commentators and pundits to drop odd tit bits such as "It I always worth noting when so and so's stable has a plunge" or "This trainer wins more than his fair share of races with his two year olds". If you make a note of these comments in the future they can prove useful and profitable information.

Another good source of information about trainers and their methods are the on course television interviews, articles and reports of stable visits that appear in the racing press. My own method is to keep a Rolodex and write down any relevant information I get about any trainer. In addition I have six trainers who I take a special interest in and monitor how they do with all their runners. As I have said before it is all about building up your knowledge. You can also gain considerable information about a trainer's current form by looking at their statistics and the "Hot" and "Cold" lists in the Racing Post.

Jockey

The jockey is not as important as the trainer in the grand scheme of things, never the less it would be foolish to overlook him or her in your deliberations. The jockeys job is to ride the horse as instructed by the trainer but that is an over simplification. Nobody would deny the brilliance of the likes of Ryan Moore, Richard Hughes, Tony McCoy or Richard Johnson who have ridden winners on horses lesser jockeys would not have even got placed. Most of the big stables have their own resident team of retained jockeys but if one of the smaller stables books a top jockey to ride one of their horses this is always worth noting.

Every season a new rising star seems to emerge from amongst the ranks of the apprentice or conditional jockeys. An apprentice jockey can claim a 7lb weight allowance until he or she has ridden 20 winners. (This can be as high as 10lb in some races if the apprentice is riding a horse from his own trainer's yard.) The allowance then drops to 5lb until they reach the 50-winner mark and after that to 3 lb. until they reach 95 winners after which they lose the allowance.

In National Hunt racing, inexperienced jockeys under the age of 26 are classed as "conditional" and in most races can claim of 7lb until they have won 15 races. After that it drops to 5 lbs. until they have won 30 races and finally to 3 lb. until their 65th success.

The value of a talented claiming jockey cannot be overrated. This can be especially true in handicap and sprint races. The booking of such a jockey by an outside stable is another point that you should note.

With the introduction of All Weather Racing in the UK in the 1990's a whole host of trainers and jockeys have targeted this particular form of the sport. Many consider All Weather an inferior form of racing, which involve poor quality horses' competing against each other with monotonous regularity. This is a little unfair but from our point of view a 4/1 winner at an All Weather track is just as good as a 4/1 winner at Royal Ascot. The point is that some jockeys have specialised in All Weather racing and have become very experienced on the various all weather surfaces. Currently Luke Morris and Adam Kirby are the jockeys to watch at the All Weather meetings.

Most jockeys are fighting a constant battle to keep their weight down and life can be very hard in this respect. Jockeys tend to have a minimum weight they can get down to, usually with the help of saunas, jogging sessions and practically starving themselves. However they normally ride at a couple of pounds heavier than their minimum weight. Therefore if you that a jockey has dropped down to his minimum weight to ride in a specific race this could indicate the stable think it has a very good chance. I have not been able to find a table of jockeys minimum weights but if you go to https://www.flatstats.co.uk/blog/jockey_minimum _riding_weight.html you will find details of the lowest weight jockeys have ridden at this season.

Courses

There are 59 racecourses in the UK including two recent additions, Ffos Las and Great Leighs, which has recently been reborn as Chelmsford City Race Course. I do not think there is anywhere in the world is there such a variety of racecourses as we have in Britain. We have round courses such as Chester, triangular shaped as at Ascot, figure of eight courses such as Fontwell and even U shaped courses like Brighton. Add to this is the fact that on some course horses race left handed and on other right handed.

Some courses are considered "easy" with a level, short run in to the winning post whilst others can be a real test of stamina with a long steep climb to the finish. There are courses with tight sharp bends, whilst others have nice gentle turns. The course can be flat or undulating and on the national hunt courses the jumps can be relatively easy or decidedly tricky.

Before you start your detailed study of a race it is worth checking out the course description. Most of the information you need for any of the 59 courses can be found at http://www.race-courses.co.uk. Once you have narrowed your selections down it can be worth revisiting the site and looking at the details of the courses on which the horse has won or run well on. Have they won or run really well on todays course or one with similar characteristics? For instance does your possible selection appear to perform better when running right handed or does it not appear to make any difference?

Visualisation

One tool in your armoury that you should not under estimate is visualisation. When you have found a possible selection go back to the formbook. Look at the runners and see if you can work out how the race will be run. Are there one or two front-runners in the field, or a horse that comes with a flourish at the end of the race? Perhaps the front-runners will have a race between themselves in the early stages and use up their energy long before the finishing post. Maybe your fancy is one of those front-runners and therefore this could be a dodgy bet.

Alternatively there may not be any front-runners in the field and none of the jockeys will want go make the pace. In this case you can imagine a slow run race, which again might or might not suit your selection. By trying to visualise the race before the off can either confirm your faith in your selection or give you cause to reconsider.

To end this chapter I will give you my personal list of RED warning lights that will stop me backing a particular horse. You may or may not agree with my list but you should draw up your own criteria for a "No bet" as this will save you a great deal of time when going through the form book.

- Never back a horse that is not proven on the going.
- Never back a horse that is unproven over the distance. (For this I consider a drop back or advance by one distance acceptable. (i.e., 5 to 6 furlongs or 1 mile up to 1 ¼ mile is OK but 5 to 7 furlongs or 1 mile to 1 ½ is not)
- Never back a horse that is unproven on the type of course that it is running on that day.
- Never back a horse whose trainer is on the "cold" list.
- Never back a horse priced at less than 3/1 and preferably 4/1 or greater.

Chapter 7

Going to the Exchange

There are probably three significant events that have changed the course of horse race betting.

1. 1794 A bookmaker called Harry Ogden set up a stall on Newmarket Heath to take bets.
2. 1961. The first licensed betting shops opened.
3. June 2000 The Betfair Exchange site was launched.

Even I am not old enough to remember Harry Ogden but as a callow youth I can easily remember those first betting shops. Originally by law they were plain, smoke blanketed unappealing places but they thrived and morphed into the comfortable betting palaces of today with their full TV coverage, coffee and tea, comfortable seating and casino machines.

Betfair was not the very first exchange site but it has grown and today is the leading betting exchange market in the world and how the punters have loved it. It has given people from all over the world, (except the USA were I believe online betting is still illegal as I write this) the chance to bet on a whole range of sports and events. For the first time punters could not only back horses to win or be placed in a race but could also lay them to lose. They could also bet "in running " if they were brave enough!! It was a revolution in horse race betting.

In this book I do not intend to go into detail on how you place bets on Betfair but if you have not used the Betfair Exchange before or would like a refresher I recommend you visit www.betting.betfair.com which is packed full of useful information and advise for the new comer.

What I want to look at the pros and cons of betting on the Betfair Exchange.

The odds offered on Betfair tend to be significantly higher than that on offer from the bookmaker and this difference tends to be even greater with the longer priced horses. Against this Betfair will take 5% commission from your winnings. This should be taken into consideration especially if you are the sort of person who backs short priced horses.

The odds on Betfair are expressed as decimal odds and this can be confusing when a punter first starts using the site. For instance decimal odds of 2.0 are the equivalent of evens. 4.50 is the same as 7/2 and odds of 36 equal 35/1.

There is no such thing as credit with Betfair so a punter has to have enough money deposited with the exchange to meet their bets when they back and any liabilities they may have when making a lay bet. This can be quite substantial if an outsider is laid to lose. For example if you think a horse priced at 21 has no chance of winning you might lay £10 on it lose but you must have £200 deposited to make this bet just to ensure the funds are there if it does by some chance win.

It is fair to say that laying long priced horse to lose can be a very risky business in the long term and is best avoided. On the Betfair system the lowest odds possible is 1.01 and the highest 1000. Normally you will only see odds of 1.01 on a horse in running at the final stage of a race and it looks a dead cert to win. Betting in running is again a service which is unique to the betting exchanges and it is possible to bet on a horse right up to the point it passes the finishing post. As you can imagine during a race a horses odds will fluctuate and it only takes a bad jump at a fence or coming slowly out of the stalls to make a significant price change. There are people who make a great deal of money from "in running" betting but equally so there a lot of gamblers who have lost a great deal of money with "in running" betting. Betting £100 to win £1 is not for the faint hearted and definitely not something I would want to do especially when Betfair are going to talk 5p from that £1 as commission. Over the years there have been some spectacular upsets and loses for punters when bets at 1.01 have come unstuck. .

In your studies you may come across the word "arbitrage" which is a term that has been taken from the financial markets and in simply means getting into a position where you cannot lose. On the Betting Exchanges it is possible to get yourself into a win-win situation quite easily. For example the favourite opens up at 3.00 but you think the price is liable to fall before the off so you back it £10 to win. It does go down to 2.25 and you then lay it for £12. If it wins you make £20 but you lose £15 on you lay bet, which gives you an over all profit of £5 less 5% so you make £4.75. If the horse loses you lose £10 on you win bet but make £12 on the lay giving you a profit of £2 less 5%.

When you look at it in black and white is all sound very easy but of course prices do not always move in the way that you expect them and as far as betting in running and arbitrage betting are concerned read and learn as much as you can and spend a month or possibly two having dry runs, paper betting before you risk any real money.

The question that is always being asked on racing and betting forums is which is best to back or lay. The argument many of the pro layers put forward is that in a 10 horse race they have 9 horses running for them as opposed to backers who only have one. This is true but layers are also carrying a much larger potential liability. As I have already stated I never like to back a horse at lower than 4/1 or at worst 3/1 but when it comes to laying the biggest price I will lay is 4/1 (5.0). Preferably I prefer to stay below the 3/1 (4.0) levels.

When it comes to backing a horse, especially at prices of 4/1(5.0) or higher, even allowing for the 5% charge Betfair offers better value that the High Street or Online Bookmakers.

Chapter 8

Can Systems Really Work?

I suspect that the majority of people who have reached Chapter Eight of this book will have almost certainly bought some type of horse race system in the past. Perhaps having been swept along by the promise of the big money that could be made using System X or System Y. Or maybe it was the list of claimed past successful results that the system had achieved that persuaded you to part with your money.

If you have had success with such a system I wish it continues to be successful for you. However, I suspect it is more likely that having purchased a system you will have lost money and by now have abandoned it.

When studying this subject it is important that we do not get hung up on the word SYSTEM. Everyone has some sort of system that they use when betting. It may be to select a certain type of horse in specific races, or an in depth study of the form of each horse in a race and only backing a runner with specific credentials. It could even be to finish work at lunchtime, have a few beers, go to the betting shop and back all the favourites until either racing finishes or you run out of money!! Even that is a system of sorts!

However, the types of systems we are talking about in this chapter are Published Systems and self generated systems.

Published Systems

There are hundreds of horse race betting systems produced every year, many created by companies and individuals whose sole object is to make money from selling these systems. If you have ever purchased a system from one of the companies or individuals you are probably bombarded with letters or emails from them on a weekly basis offering the very latest sure fire, cannot fail system. The sad fact is that none of their systems are likely to work for you. There are a number of reasons for this:

The systems are not tested thoroughly enough. One expert Michael Wilding the author of the excellent Puntology course maintains that you should monitor a system for a year, then paper test it for another 6 months before risking your money on it. He is of course totally right but I doubt if there are many of us who would have the patience to do that.

Many systems are created using what is called back fitting. This is the process of checking the system and make it fit against past results. The problem with this is that when the results do not quite match the system the compilers created they just add further variables. It is a bit like tipping a horse after it has won.

A successful and well-advertised system can sell thousands of copies and if a thousand punters start following the method the price of the horse indicated by the system will fall. This fact alone can turn what was potentially a profitable system into an unprofitable one. This is the reason why so often a system you bought works perfectly well until you start putting your money down and then it all goes pear shaped.

Other than the get rich merchants there is one other type of system creator. These are honest individuals who love the sport of horse racing and the act of betting. They have spent many lonely hours study statistics, form, breeding and all the other factors that can help identify prospective winners. They then publish the system in all good faith and it works well for a while but then hits a bad patch. We the betting masses abandon it in droves and move on to the next "Great System". If you have ever purchased a system like this I will give you one piece of advice after six months or a year go back and try it again. Good horse race systems just like punters will hit loosing streaks but it is surprising how often they can come back and prove profitable once more. Having said that all racing systems have a life expectancy. Nothing in life ever stays the same and that is just as true in horse racing, over time the conditions and statistics that the system relies upon will have changed and it will be no longer workable.

Racing systems can cost anything from a few pence, (99p on eBay) up to many hundreds of pounds. There are even seminars that cost up to £6,000 that will teach you specific systems and betting methods.

Are they worth it?

Who can say? Possibly the people who have bought them but I suspect that very few would pass the value for money test. If you were considering buying a horse race betting system these are the points I would consider.

- Have the claims on past results been tested by an independent source?

- Are there any independent reviews of the system on the Internet? Typing the system name into your browser and seeing what comes up is an easy way to check this. However, beware of review sites that have a link back to the system sales page because they will almost certainly be on a commission for any sales made coming from that link. This makes it highly unlikely that their review will be totally unbiased.

- Check to see if the seller provides basic facts in their advertisement such as a contact address or telephone number. It is all right promising money back guarantees but if there is no way of contacting the seller these can be worthless.

- If you have any questions about the system try and contact the seller for an answer. If none is forth coming it should tell you everything you need to know about whether to buy or not.

- Quite often the advertising will claim big figure profits such as £2000 a month profit. Check what staking level this is based on. Usually £100 per bet is quoted but if your maximum bet is £10 that £2000 will come down to £200 even if the claim is truthful so bare that in mind. Another point regarding staking is that if a system will not work using level stakes then I believe it should be avoided.

An alternative and much cheaper option is to create your own system.

Your own system

A system is basically a set of rules that you stick to in the expectation that by doing so you will make a profit from your horse race betting activity. The reason that you expect to make that profit is because either you or someone else has research the data and statistics and decided that by using this information you can make a return for your efforts.

That all sounds very simple which is not surprising because the golden rule about devising any horse race system should be to KEEP IT SIMPLE?

The more variables and rules that you put into a system the more there is to go wrong.

The first step to creating your own system is to begin with an assumption. The next stage is to carry out some research to test that assumption. Let me give you an example let us start with that old chestnut, "In a 3 horse race, always back the outsider". How often have you heard someone say that at the races or in the betting shop?

So the system is simply

1. Exclude all amateur, apprentice and ladies races.

2. 3 Runner races only

3. Back the outsider in the betting.

Back in 2010 www.flatstats.co.uk checked back over 182 3 horse races and discovered that out of the 182 races the outsider only won 21 times giving a 11.5% strike rate and as a result you would have lost 62.4% of your betting bank.

This may not look too promising but it might be worth digging a little further. The above statistics are based on bookies starting prices. However, we already know that the odds on Betfair are usually better especially for higher priced horses. Perhaps if we added an extra variable

4. Back the outside to win on Betfair

This might go some way to making this a profitable system. Possibly is you removed all races where the favourite started odds on you could discover that you got a better return or perhaps just the reverse and you would find that the outsider won more often when the favourite was odds on. Whatever the result of your researches this could give you another variable,

This would be as far as I would go with this assumption, remember we are trying to keep it simple and five variables is more than enough. There are plenty of web sites that can provide the information that you need to build your systems. I have already mentioned www.flatstats.co.uk and another that I will recommend is www.horseracebase.com. This last one offers a free 3 day trial so you can test it out and after that you can use it for as little as £12.50 per month which is considerably cheaper than some of the other data sites.

By necessity systems are based on the statistics from past events and as in any statistical calculation the larger the sample the greater the accuracy of the figures produced. For example if you tossed a coin we know that the odds on it landing heads up is 50% as there are only two options it can either land heads up or tails up.

Now if you tossed that same coin 10 times it might land 6 times heads and 4 times tails. That does not mean based on this information you could back heads all the time and win 6 times and lose 4 thereby making a profit of 20% on every ten tosses.

This system would fail because 10 is too small a sample to provide a significant result. It is almost certain if you continued this test for a thousand tosses the result would be nearer 50/50 heads and tails. The same rule applies when you develop your own systems, the greater the sample the more likely you are to produce reliable results.

If you create your own system make it specific. By that I mean there is no system that works across all facets of horse racing. Produce a system for flat races, hurdles, chases or all weather but not one that covers them all. . You may even want to specialize even further in say 2 year olds, novice chases, handicap or non-handicap races. Your system could be based on specific trainers or another factor such as distance traveled to the meeting or days since last run. There are no limits to the factors you can work on to find a profitable system.

Once you have produced your first system the question come, how long you should test it before "going live" and start betting with real money. As I mentioned before Michael Wilding has suggested that you should spend a year monitoring the results, then six months paper testing before taking the plunge if all has gone well. This is good advice but I know that it is not something I could wait that long to try. I would paper test from day one and if all looked good after six months I would start betting. Just to make it clear paper testing is making your selections, taking a note of it and checking the results without actually putting any money on them. This can be a little frustrating when the winners start going in but a great relief when and if the system proves not to be as good as you hoped.

How to use systems

No matter how good a system is there will come a time when it begins to fail. This can come about for a variety of reasons:

1. The system has a basic flaw in its assumptions.

2 So many people start using it that it affects the prices and the system loses its edge.

3. The circumstances that the system is based on change. For example a course improves its drainage system and the advantage to low drawn runners disappears.

4. The system simply has a losing run and punters quickly lose faith and give up on it.

If there is a flaw in a system this will quickly become apparent and providing you have tested it before risking your money it will not be out of pocket by too much.

Any horse race system is designed to give the punter an edge over the bookmaker and effectively turn the odds in his or her favour. If too many start backing the same horse because the system indicates it then this can affect the horse's odds and the punters can lose the edge and the system becomes unprofitable.

It is quite possible that you may discover a fact such as horses running from the outside draw rarely win sprint races on a certain track. This may lead you to devise a system to lay the outside runner. Then the racecourse executive decides to move the stalls across to the other side of the track and the situation changes. It is also worth realizing that if you have noticed it is pretty certain that the bookies will not be too slow to notice it as well and this will be reflected in the horse's price again losing you the edge.

Every racing system just like every punter is going to have a losing run and if this happens the typical reaction of most punters is to abandon the system and throw it into a corner never to see the light of day again. Obviously if a system starts losing consistently you should give it a rest or possibly revert to paper testing but don't abandon it forever. I have several systems which I have revived a year or two later and found that they have started to work well again.

The trouble with many punters is that they are looking for an easy way to find winners and make money. This is why creating and selling horse race systems is such a profitable business. If there is an easy way to make money other than profiting from the online bookies bonuses then I have yet to find it.

If you find either a tipster or system that consistently provides you with profitable betting opportunities you are very lucky. When you see an advert in the racing press or on the Internet offering a system that claims a 70%+ success rate do you not wonder why the guy is selling it. Let's face it if I could guarantee that kind of success rate I would not be bothered to sell it and risk it losing it's edge for £10 or £20.

 In my experience the key to success is not using systems but training yourself to adopt a systematic or methodical approach to find your selections. That means that you know what you want to achieve, you select the races that give you the best opportunity to find a winner in the right price range. You then study the form to find the horses capable of winning the race and then try to narrow that down to one selection. If that is not possible you discard the race and move on. Always be aware that there will be days when there is no obvious selection whilst on another day there might be two or three. This is not a system;

it is just adopting systematic or methodical approach.

Tipsters

I have never seriously used a Tipster service. My basic concern is that anyone can set up as a tipster and so why should you give some unknown person money just for sending you the name of some horses. Never the less, I know people who have had considerable success using some tipster services.

There are some honest, knowledgeable, hard working and successful men and women providing good tipping services. What they are effectively doing is saving you the time and effort to do your own study and research. How you find these good tipsters can be very hit and miss unless someone you trust recommends someone.

Personally I cannot recommend any tipster because I do not have personal experience of any. However, you have to realize that if you place all your faith in any tipster you are going to be totally reliant upon them. If they retire or simply go out of business you are back where you started.

Build up your own knowledge base, gain experience and trust your own judgment and you will be reliant upon nobody. In other words you will be able to *"catch your own fish"*

Chapter Nine

The Winning Post

If this book were a horse race we would be fast approaching the winning post. In other words we are reaching the end and I hope that you have learnt something that you can take with you to improve your chances of coming out ahead of the bookmaker.

It is not an easy task but the rewards can be well worth the challenge. You will at times need to keep the faith, which in some ways is just as important as keeping good records. Money management is also of key importance as is a wealth of knowledge. A few years ago I heard a leading business guru state that if you spent an hour a day reading books on your specialist subject, within 3 years you would become an expert. If you continue for another two years you would become a world expert. How true that is I don't know, but I am sure that the more that you know about horse racing and betting the more you are likely to profit.

If you have not yet started the first course of action is to start collecting the bookies bonuses and build up your betting pot. While you are doing this you should start collecting and reading books on the various aspects of horse race betting. The Racing Post publishes some very good ones and details can be found on their web site. Much of my own library was build up from books, (often purchased second hand) from Amazon and eBay.

You may find it useful to reread this book and start paper testing some of your selections. Remember if you only select horses priced at 4/1 or higher a success rate of over 25% will show you a profit.

I wish you all good fortune.

A Final Point

The methods I have outlined will normally produce only one to three bets a day. This is controlled gambling, but unfortunately there are people whose lives have been ruined by becoming uncontrolled gamblers. If you think there is any chance that this could or has happened to you then throw this book into the waste bin and walk away. Gambling can ruin lives please bet responsibly.

Disclaimer

The information provided in this e-book is to the best of the authors and publishers knowledge accurate and true. It is based on the experiences and studies carried out by the author. However, whilst every effort has been made to ensure the accuracy of the content neither the author nor publishers will accept any responsibility either directly or indirectly related to the content contained in this book.

We have made no claims as to any

specific potential financial gain that could result from horse race betting. Any form of gambling carries an inherent risk of loss and this should be realised by anyone placing a wager or bet.

Horse racing is not a get quick rich scheme and should not be treat as such. It is up to each individual to exercise due caution and diligence when gambling.

It is always possible to lose as well as win when betting and no one should bet more than they can afford to lose.

My Book List

As you will have gathered I am a great believer in increasing my knowledge by reading books about horse racing, betting and systems. To finish is book I am going to list 10 books from my library that I have found interesting or useful. Many of them will by now out of print but you should be able to find copies on Amazon, eBay or in your local charity shop or car boot sale.

Braddock's Complete Guide To Horse, Racing. Selection & Betting. By Peter Braddock.

Betting for a living by Nick Mordin

Winning without Thinking by Nick Mordin

The Complete Manual of Racing & Betting Systems by David Duncan

The Definitive Guide to Betting Exchanges edited by Paul Kealy

Winning on Betfair for Dummies by Jack Houghton

The Punters Friend by Jack Waterman

The Betting Edge by David Lee-Priest

Betting on the All Weather by David Bellingham

The Winning Streak by Peter Graham

17022504R00070

Printed in Great Britain
by Amazon